The way Home

The way Home

Finding where we belong

Ron Kallmier

CWR

Published 2017 by CWR, Waverley Abbey House, Waverley Lane, Farnham, Surrey GU9 8EP, UK.
CWR is a Registered Charity – Number 294387 and a Limited Company registered in England – Registration Number 1990308.

For a list of National Distributors, visit www.cwr.org.uk/distributors

Concept development, editing, design and production by CWR.
Every effort has been made to ensure that this book contains the correct permissions and references, but if anything has been inadvertently overlooked the Publisher will be pleased to make the necessary arrangements at the first opportunity. Please contact the Publisher directly.
Cover image: CWR
Printed in the UK by Linney.
ISBN: 978-1-78259-096-5

Acknowledgements

I would like to express my grateful appreciation to the people who kindly submitted their life stories to become part of this book. Without them, this book would not be possible. I would also like to thank the CWR editorial team for their patience, as this project has unfolded over several years.

Jeanette, my wife and my best friend, has stood by me through the writing process and I am truly grateful for her support. Undoubtedly there are other people I should thank who have made a variety of contributions to this book, but I trust I can acknowledge their contributions face-to-face at some point.

I am grateful to God for the opportunity to write this book. I pray that it will be an aid to some of us who are on the journey of discovering God.

I am indebted to the following authors for their insights into the culture and background of what is commonly called the 'Parable of the Prodigal Son' (Luke 15):

- Timothy Keller, *The Prodigal God* (London: Hodder & Stoughton, 2008)
- Kenneth E Bailey, *Jacob and the Prodigal* (Downers Grove, IL, USA: IVP, 2003)
- Kenneth E Bailey, *Jesus Through Middle-Eastern Eyes* (Downers Grove, IL, USA: IVP, 2008)

Any unintended errors in culture or background are fully my responsibility.

Some of the names of the biography authors have been changed to protect the identity of the other people mentioned in their stories. Other stories included are based on my own experiences, or information I have received.

Contents

Introduction

Throughout human history, it seems that life has always been a struggle. But being human in the twenty-first century is tough, and the issues that we are facing seem to be increasingly unique to the age in which we live. We look at the wider world around us and then up close at some of the challenges and struggles that we know we must confront. There are many things that we would like to change, but we often feel powerless to do so.

Most of us want to feel we are secure people who are significant to others, and whose lives make some sort of difference in the world – no matter how small that difference may be. But our planet is battered by war, and the grinding poverty, disease and displacement that too many of our fellow human beings suffer. Constantly in touch with the latest news updates, we are all too aware of the dangers and threats that exist, which could destroy our present or our future security. The news isn't often all that good. Add to this the more immediate challenges and trials of our personal situations, and we see that the world is definitely not a safe or predictable place.

There must be more than this.

Through the decades of my working life as an educator, leader, pastor and counsellor, I have often come into contact with people in the midst of life's crises. As I consider my own life, and the lives of the thousands of people I have met, I have come to believe that there exists in all of us a deep longing to find a rock-solid security in something, or someone. We want to be whole and we want to be safe. We want to live freely and well.

If you were to ask ten people what life is all about, you would most likely get ten different answers. If we're honest, most of us probably don't spend too much time trying to understand the deep questions about meaning and purpose – we just get on with our lives the best we can and make the best of our circumstances. But even if we think we're contented with not having the answers, every now and again we're reminded of some of life's big questions: Why was I born? Does my life have any meaning? Why do I feel different to others? Where do I belong? Am I just an accident, or does my existence have a purpose? Why do I struggle with problems and pain? Is there a God? If there is a God, what is He like?

This book is written to invite you to explore some of these questions, and to help you consider what you really think about purpose, identity, security and God. In this book you will find the real stories of a number of individuals who, in the struggles of their lives, have discovered God for themselves. They are all very different, and each writer sees God somewhat differently. They are all still on the journey of discovery of themselves and of understanding God better. I am grateful that each one agreed to invite us to see things from their perspective.

But one thing that each of these stories has in common is the search for our creator. In the process, each person has been led on a unique pathway, growing in their understanding of God. Some of their histories have been extremely painful, even traumatic. Each one still faces challenges in their lives now. These experiences have shaped their thoughts and their very lives, and the way their journeys towards God have unfolded. Like our storytellers, your story is unique also. But I am hopeful that as you read and reflect on these pages, you will be motivated to go deeper in your own search for your creator.

There is another story included here too – a very old story that helps to tie all the other together. It is a story told by Jesus the Messiah, a master teacher, who Christians believe is the Son of God. Jesus told the story of 'the prodigal son' to help those who heard Him teach to understand God – His Father – as our Father too. Jesus told this story to describe the true attitude of God towards ordinary people like us, people who are sometimes confused and a little lost in their lives. The Father that Jesus describes in this story is the kindest, most loving and forgiving father anyone could hope to find. His story paints a very different understanding of God from the commonly held view of His time, and is probably a very different view to the one many people have today.

Something we all need to consider is our own view of God. Where did our view of God come from? How has this view of God influenced our lives? Do we need to rethink our ideas? This book aims to take us on a journey of discovery of our human origins, through a better understanding of our deep longings for that which only our creator can satisfy. It is my belief that He desires to be the solid ground for our lives, even when life itself is so unpredictable.

Part One:
Life Journeys

01

The shaping of you and me

'Nothing in life is to be feared, it is only to be understood. Now is the time to understand more, so that we may fear less.'

Marie Curie

It goes without saying that we have absolutely no control over many things in our early lives: when we are born; our natural parents; whether we are welcomed or rejected as babies; what culture and social status we find ourselves in; whether our early years are warm and safe, or harmful and overshadowed with insecurity and fear.

Whatever our roots and our background, we endeavour to adapt and to try to make sense of what life is all about. As we grow, we begin to ask some of life's big questions: Who am I? Why am I here? What does my life mean? How do I find my way to a successful life? Of course, many of us find ourselves in difficult circumstances from birth: circumstances and environments that warp our sense of identity and possibility.

Selina's early life was far from ideal. Unloved and abandoned from her earliest years, she recounts a remarkable journey leading to a sense of purpose and identity that seemed highly improbable from her infant years. Inevitably, and like so many of us, she still carries some emotional scars from her childhood.

Selina

What does adoption mean to me?

Acceptance, approval, blessing, love, a sense of belonging, purpose.

A child or adult who is accepted and made part of a family that they were not born into – they are a part of a new family. This is exactly what God did in my life.

As a toddler I was left on a train, and was adopted

from an orphanage in Sri Lanka at age four and brought up in Australia. I officially became part of a new, big family, who love me – and whom I love. There is no mistaking who God chose as my family, but what I didn't always know is that I have an extended family that is far bigger than I could ever imagine.

I went to a Christian school and I believed in Jesus. I had been to church on and off in my life and I listened to some Christian music (I even sat with my tape player and would record the music), but I wanted to be a part of the crowd. I really struggled sometimes as I just wanted to belong: to feel included, accepted and loved. During this time there were various teachers who would encourage me, and as I look back, I see how God sowed seeds of faith into my life.

Sometimes we wonder why people who have been such an important part of our lives are no longer there. This was certainly my experience when I left school and lost touch with a lot of my friends. But it says in the Bible: 'God places the lonely in families; he sets the prisoners free and gives them joy' (Psalm 68:6, NLT). God has put Christian people in my life at every stage – school, university, work – confirming that He's there. He has said, 'Never will I leave you; never will I forsake you' (Hebrews 13:5). There were Christian friends and certain family members who invited me to church events and conferences, and they really challenged me. I came to realise that God really was with me as I went through various trials in my everyday life.

Eventually, I started looking for a church. It was

a time of learning, growing and being challenged. I wanted to know where I belonged. I knew God was in my life. I had the 'head knowledge' of knowing Jesus, but in terms of knowing in my heart it was, and still is, a continuing journey. I longed to go back to Sri Lanka, and God gave me that opportunity a few years ago. Once I went, I would not be the same again.

Sri Lanka was confronting and challenging, but I learned so much more about Jesus. I realised that I was searching for something – searching for a sense of belonging, identity, love, peace and comfort that only God can provide, as He created me and knows me better than I even know myself.

Once back from Sri Lanka, I found a home at a church that taught me about prayer, generosity and unconditional love – that I am loved, to love myself, and to see myself as God sees me. I have a sense of belonging, and a purpose to reach communities and nations for Jesus.

A couple of years ago my mum and I were in a major car accident. The car flipped on its roof, leaving us hanging upside down inside. Miraculously, my mum had no serious injuries, and I had no injuries apart from the fact that the top of my head and knee were sore. This event made me realise that God is a miracle-working God. Why would He save my life if He didn't have a purpose? I remember around that time – before the accident – I had been asking God why He had even put me here on this earth and what my purpose was.

Sometime after that, I was given the opportunity to

go to India on a mission trip with an organisation called Hope Global. At that time I'd had no plans to go to India. But I went to church one Sunday and, India was up on the screen – Hope Global were taking a mission team there. Immediately I felt that God was prodding me to check it out, so I applied – and was accepted! In India we visited a lot of orphanages and I shared my story. It was challenging and inspiring. A mixture of emotions ran through me. India was more of a blessing than words can describe.

My time in India really gave me a heart for reaching out to people in other countries. When I came back, I worked for a well-known NGO (Non-Government Organisation) where my role meant I would meet people from many nations. I believe that through this time, God has given me a greater compassion for all nations, not just India or Sri Lanka. What I have seen and heard gives me a greater desire to understand God's heartbeat for people all over the world.

The last few months have been very hard for me, and, if I'm honest, have really challenged my faith. I felt that my time at the church I was going to was coming to an end, and so I made the decision to leave (I have since been attending a different church). I also faced challenges in my workplace with bullying and confronted the issue with a formal complaint, which took a great emotional toll – but I was always aware that God would never leave me, and He didn't. His promise is that He will never leave or forsake us.

But still, my faith was challenged in every way.

I made a very tough decision to leave my job. I believe God gave me a peace about leaving and I was able to finish well. Even though I felt like giving up, God sent me really good friends who continued to support and love me, and speak positive and affirming things over me. I'm also very grateful for my adoptive family, who were always there for me.

I feel that God is slowly mending my heart again. He wants me to remember His love; that He is the beginning and the end. He is my comforter; my counsellor; my strength and my peace. I am discovering that we shouldn't limit Him, and that I can dream big – all things are possible with Him!

In my experience, faith is a journey on which you grow, learn, overcome... grow, learn, overcome. I would say that I still go into default mode and ask, 'Where do I belong?', especially now that I'm in a season of transition, but in God's strength, I have come this far. I am learning not to limit Him – He continually reminds me of His faithfulness. He has given me purpose.

There are many intriguing gaps in Selina's eventful life story here, aren't there? Imagine the shock and trauma any infant would feel when they realised that they were on a train and that their parents had abandoned them.

'I had been asking God why He had even put me here on this earth and what my purpose was.'

Much like Selina's story, happily there are many reports of abandoned or neglected children being adopted into loving, caring families. These children may still have roots in the loss of their biological parents, but they have an environment where they feel safe. However, there are simply too many accounts of children who, adopted or not, have through no fault of their own found themselves in situations of neglect, bullying, and even abuse of all types. Sadly, there are just too many of us who have learned to survive in unsafe and hostile home environments. Perhaps this is your experience.

Does our human life have a greater meaning than merely going through the motions of existence? Some would say yes, life does have meaning and purpose. Others would disagree. But whichever view we take, our lives are shaped by our conclusions about why we are here on earth, whether by chance or design. Having read or heard many of the arguments for and against the existence of God, it now appears to me that something more than logic and argument is required to resolve this mystery.

There are many things about life on this planet that go beyond 'reason' and 'logic'. A father looks at his new-born baby for the first time and bursts into tears of joy. A spectacular sunset displays its magnificent colour patterns around the horizon, enthralling those watching. Magnificent pieces of music stir our emotions. Are all these things acts of chance? Can reason, argument or science alone provide the answers to our deep longings, to our problems and emotional pain?

And what of love? It's hard to define or to explain,

but love is so essential to the human soul. Where does love come from? Is it merely a trick of human psychology? There is something deep within our humanity that believes that we deserve more. We want fulfilment. We want respect. We crave security and we desire to belong. We want our lives to have value. We also have an inbuilt intense sense of justice and injustice. Where do these desires come from? Why are they present in us? Did God shape our humanity with these desires as an essential part of who we are as people?

Selina is convinced that it was God who was steering her life, even during the most threatening and confusing of times. If she has been misled in her faith in God and we are merely the products of chance, then the ideas of us being on earth for a purpose, of our having personal rights, of justice, and of our worth as individuals, are all very sad tricks of the evolutionary process. If we have not been created by a divine being, we are simply a random accident, making the most of what we have, hoping to achieve a pleasant existence, but inevitably coming to a very final end of our lives.

But Selina presents us with an alternative view of life. Her God-given heart for the nations gave her a sense of justice, love, family and acceptance. The context of this is within her identity as a created and loved human being – and this awareness of her true identity has transformed her world-view.

02

Life's big questions

'I have seen the burden God has laid on the human race. He has made everything beautiful in its time. He has also set eternity in the human heart; yet no one can fathom what God has done from beginning to end.'

Ecclesiastes 3:10–11

A teenage girl approached a Christian youth worker in a coffee shop. Having heard some of his conversation about God, life and Christianity, she wanted to challenge the youth worker by presenting her own view on the meaning of life.

'Do you want to hear my life's story?' she asked the youth worker over a coffee.

'Sure,' he replied.

'It's very short,' she cautioned.

'That's OK,' he said, now quite curious.

'Well, here it is,' she said, and then paused for a moment before speaking. 'Born today. Died tomorrow. Lived in between. That's my life.'

Hers was a simple statement that summarised her beliefs about her existence. Her message was clear: life is brief, and then it's over.

How would you have responded to her? How would you describe the meaning of your life in one sentence?

Michael is someone else who has struggled with the meaning of his existence. From an early age he was confronted with similar questions about meaning and purpose, life and death.

Michael

I come from a middle-income Asian family. Both of my parents worked – Mum was a teacher, and Dad a manager. We had no practising religion, although I found out later that my mum had been baptised in a Christian church as a teenager. I grew up using the term 'free-thinker', and was pretty proud to announce it every time I was asked.

My grandparents were rooted in traditional ancestor worship. During religious festivities, I would do as they asked – take a joss (incense) stick, clasp it in my hand and pray towards the heavens, or sometimes at the food offered to the ancestors. Another ritual involved the burning of incense papers to appease the gods and ancestor spirits. This was the 'seventh month' in the Chinese lunar calendar, when supposedly the hell gates were opened and all the spirits were allowed to roam free. The sacrifices of incense and food were so that the spirits were satisfied and would not come in search of the living – avoiding unnecessary 'encounters'. So I grew up with a fear of unknown spirits and gods, in a culture drenched in superstition.

I first heard about Christianity when I went to a Christian nursery school. I remember stories being told of the baby Moses drifting down some river in a basket. (I would often confuse this baby with the baby Jesus, which I remembered as the story associated with Christmas.) When I was about ten, I began to question the meaning of life. I vividly remember looking out of the kitchen window (in our sixth-floor flat), and wondering what would happen to me if I jumped to my death. From that time my thinking was influenced by various suicide cases that I'd heard about – once I actually witnessed the aftermath of one very bloody floor after a body had been removed. It was mostly old people who leapt to their death, I was told.

I wondered about my life – finishing school, getting a job, getting married, having children, having grandchildren, growing old and sick, then dying... it seemed pretty meaningless. If all we had to look forward to was death, then why not now? Why waste time? By that age, I had some concept of reincarnation through my Buddhist influences. I was told that one had to do good to earn certain rights to a better reincarnation. My biggest fear was to be reincarnated as a cockroach. It was not something I readily accepted, but the uncertainty of it all kept me from ending my life.

Back at the kitchen window, I always prayed to 'God', just speaking, asking and wondering in my head. Sometimes, I would pray for the safety of my parents, because I dreaded the thought of being orphaned should they die in an accident. I sensed that there was a 'God' out there; a supreme being who could hear my thoughts, and that this 'God' was not the same one that I prayed to with the joss stick.

As a teenager I went to a missionary school, and that was where Christianity was first explained to me. I found the Christian explanation of the afterlife reasonable enough, and I did not want to go to hell, for sure – so I was very ready to confess my sins, ask for forgiveness in Christ, and be assured of a ticket to heaven after I died. I felt it was a done deal, and I was happy for some time. I began to attend church and participated in youth activities, Bible studies, church camps and so on.

I thought I was a pretty good Christian: obedient, well-behaved, and respectful. It was only in my late teens and as a young adult that I started struggling with the moral issues of sexuality, and certain other things that Christianity called 'sin'. There began my real struggle, despite the fact that I was still faithfully attending church.

There were more struggles through adulthood, and I carried a deep sense of guilt and hypocrisy as I tried to hide my sin. The mounting pressures of career and family added to the stress. I kept going to God to ask for forgiveness, but failed again and again. I struggled with something inside of me telling me that I was hopeless and would never be good enough for God.

Finally, through a Bible study programme that my church was running, I began to understand a different side of the Christian faith. I finally understood that God's love and forgiveness were unconditional. I learned the difference between guilt and repentance, condemnation and forgiveness. That was the beginning of a journey of transformation and of changing my thinking. I began to realise the meaning of God's amazing grace and ability to forgive someone like me. Ironically, in my earlier days of faith, I never felt that I was that sinful. Then, as I had grown up, I had felt that I could never be forgiven for repeatedly failing God.

It has been about ten years since that turning point in my life. God has been gracious, patient, loving, and gently changing me to understand and live according to His purpose. The journey has proven God to be one who is ever faithful. As I surrender more and more, God never ceases to amaze more and more.

'I wondered about my life – finishing school, getting a job, getting married, having children, having grandchildren, growing old and sick, then dying... it seemed pretty meaningless. If all we had to look forward to was death, then why not now? Why waste time?'

Are our lives simply one big evolutionary mistake? Human intelligence is somehow tuned to explore the very questions that Michael struggled with. Other creatures simply exist and then die, but for some reason, as humans, we want to know *why* we are here. If this is a mechanism that we have supposedly evolved, it is an ironic one – why would we 'evolve' to become hardwired to discover our own intrinsic pointlessness? That would indeed be a cruel trick of the evolutionary process; surely it would be better if we could avoid such hopeless thinking. And further to the question of purpose, it appears that thinking about the past and the future is unavoidable for humans. When life is overwhelming, we can become reduced to living one day at a time, because thinking and planning ahead seems so futile. Is this all there is?

Interestingly, most young children seem to have no problem with the idea of God, no matter how fuzzy their ideas are. Many abandon these beliefs later. Some move on to a deeper understanding of the deity they follow and develop a personal faith. Others embrace the arguments and position of atheism or agnosticism – they don't believe in God any longer, or they say they simply do not know what to believe. In most major world religions, there is a key element of struggle and striving: the belief that we need to make ourselves good enough. Others may follow their religious systems to try to make their lives work well and to avoid the actions of evil spirits. Michael knew this only too well.

It seems that a life without God gives us two options: make your own rules and find your own way, or come under the influence and control of nasty spiritual beings and their desires. But is there another foundation for finding meaning and direction to life? Michael's journey suggests there is. What is interesting in Michael's story is how he came to sense the presence of a supreme God; a God whom he recognised as different from all the spirit beings his family and ancestors worshipped and feared.

'I sensed that there was a "God" out there; a supreme being who could hear my thoughts, and that this "God" was not the same one that I prayed to with the joss stick.'

Many of us will find our own way and try to give meaning to our lives. But when we come to the point of recognising our limitations, some of us are drawn to the idea of a supreme being. Often it is in times of major crisis that a person will cry out to 'God', though they may have never given God any serious thought in the past. Michael was brought up in a religion that worshipped ancestral and other spirits for self-protection and for a better life after death in reincarnation. But despite his cultural and religious background, he held to the idea of a supreme God who was beyond what he knew. How did this happen? I believe that deep within each of us, there is the idea of a supreme being – God, if you like. Even more, I believe we are drawn to the idea of finding our way to God, to know Him and to find what we are seeking through Him and in Him.

Many of us may have learned to reject the idea of God because we have been taught that religion is a crutch, or that the idea of God is a fable used to control the masses. Sadly, many religious leaders have used their ideas about God to control those under their influence. But do these abuses and failures in human religious leaders mean that God does not exist? It was a question that I struggled with for a period of time in my life.

Raised in a conservative Christian household, I was brought up to believe in God and to follow the beliefs of my parents. As a teenager, I met many young people my age who lived for fun and personal fulfilment, with no thoughts about God. But it was in my first year of studying philosophy at university that I started to examine my Christian beliefs more closely. My comfortable world-view was disturbed in my first philosophy lecture in a crowded lecture theatre. In his opening words, the professor challenged those of us who believed in God to stand up. I counted three of us on our feet. Maybe some students were too embarrassed or too wary to join in. There was no way of telling.

The professor spent a considerable amount of time mocking our beliefs. I was red-faced, shocked and very embarrassed. He devoted the rest of that semester to prove by 'logic' that God could not exist. This was a very confusing time for me as I struggled with two contradictory views of life and the world: one with God at the centre, and the alternative view that there is no such being as God.

Without going into all the details of my thinking at that time, I have to say that looking back, I am so pleased that I was challenged to rethink my views and my values. On reflection, I am reasonably confident that many students simply had the views they brought to university confirmed – that God does not exist, or alternatively, that God is not relevant to their lives. Others in that class may have lost their faith as a result. Others may have been unsettled by the professor's absolute view, and been moved to explore further. I don't know. But for me, looking back on the embarrassment and the confusion of that philosophy class, I realised how much I benefitted from being challenged with a different view concerning what it means to be human. I was able to recognise why others held different world-views to me. My faith in what I believed about God was modified a little, and my faith foundations became stronger. My beliefs were more refined, more mature and more settled than they had been before. A little while after that philosophy class was over, I could truly say that I was pleased to have gone through the experience.

Michael's journey began in childhood with a belief in many gods. He came to an inner awareness of one supreme being who he came to know as his creator, his God. Of course, this was a gradual process. Such a big shift in world-views involves a journey – a process – rather than a sudden change. This was indeed Michael's experience, as it was for me.

I trust that as you continue to read, you too will be challenged and encouraged to look at what you have always believed, and perhaps to think again – to think differently about your life, and about God.

03

The search for significance

'See what great love the Father has lavished on us, that we should be called children of God! And that is what we are! The reason the world does not know us is that it did not know him.'

1 John 3:1

One of the greatest challenges of being human is finding a way to overcome negative thoughts and emotions. As infants we may be unable to understand and explain what is happening in our immediate surroundings, but we store the images, emotions and experiences. We form memories based on how we perceive life works for us. As life progresses, our self-image and view of the world become more firmly established as we reflect on our past and our present.

Relationships play an important part in how we understand ourselves. Warm, positive, secure and nurturing relationships help us to say to ourselves, 'I am OK.' But when our early relationships produce abuse, insecurity, shame or unworthiness, our self-image suffers accordingly. Most of us will encounter a mixture of helpful and harmful relationship experiences throughout life. For example, we may feel safe at home, but school may be a hostile environment where we face bullying, failure or loneliness. In addition to our relationships, we gradually build up a picture of what it means to be successful by observing and listening to others. Thrown into the mix is what the media and popular culture have to say about success. Perhaps we constantly remember the words of parents/teachers: 'You can do better' or 'You're useless!'

While many thrive in their early years, others do not. Some of us develop a sense of inadequacy because of our poor performance in schoolwork. Some of us may feel inferior because of our failures to build positive relationships with others. Some of us may struggle to compete with our peers in physical activities such as sports. It can be easy to measure ourselves by how we *believe* others see us – our perception of the opinions of others. It is our perceptions, rather than reality, that drive our thoughts and feelings and behaviour.

It is so easy to see ourselves as failures – as inadequate and insignificant – when we engage in negative self-talk. This is made worse if our social contacts are not supportive and nurturing.

Greg's experience is an example of this, but his painful beginning leads to a positive outcome. His story leads us into the inner world of a person who struggled with a common human problem – shyness. Like so many people, Greg's problem was not physically life threatening but it invaded his thought life and his emotions continually. It was like a great emotional weight that he carried into every life situation, unable to break out of his sense of inadequacy. His desire to overcome his shyness and be accepted by others was the trigger that eventually propelled Greg on a journey of God discovery.

Greg

I was painfully shy as a teenager. My face was scarred by severe acne, so I was very self-conscious and totally lacking self-confidence. Like most teenagers, I felt I was the only one with social and physical inadequacies. I longed to fit in with the crowd at school, to be liked, to have good looks and a manly physique, to get into the rugby team, to be confident in the company of girls without being tongue-tied, to be accepted and loved for who I was despite my facial blemishes and uninteresting (or so I assumed) personality. But that doesn't tend to happen when you're as shy as I was.

With both parents working all day, and having no siblings and few friends, I spent many hours outdoors on my own. I felt very lonely and isolated. I had so many unanswered questions about the meaning of life and my existence. The country I lived in was going through a civil war, and when I turned 18 I would be conscripted into the army to fight for reasons I didn't even understand. There were thousands of questions spinning in my young mind, all demanding answers.

My classmates would talk about people and events of interest and the usual stuff teenagers often fixate on. Even religion occasionally came up for debate at lunch breaks, and for the first time, I started thinking about God. I listened more than argued because I had no understanding about such things.

The 'in' crowd at school were regularly going to Friday night bars and clubs, and stories of how much alcohol was consumed (and other exploits) were routinely reported back to the class on Monday mornings. I was envious, but too shy to participate. I desperately wanted to go out on Friday nights – anywhere! – but sat alone at home. So when some of my friends invited me to a church youth group on Friday nights, I jumped at the offer. Anything for a night out!

I was welcomed and accepted for who I was, and was soon making new friends my own age (including girls!). We had loads of fun playing crazy games, singing and discussing life issues. For the first time I heard about Jesus' life and death on a cross. The relaxed environment meant I could ask and get honest answers to my burning questions. Over the next few months my friends and I had endless discussions at school about Jesus, the Bible, and faith. I asked plenty of questions about God and the answers began to make sense.

One Friday evening I found myself at a huge Christian event at a national stadium, and again I heard the message of Jesus preached. Right then, I just knew I had to trust Jesus as my Saviour. The moment I made that decision, I experienced the most amazing sense of relief and peace. At the invitation to come forward, I stood and calmly walked from the top tier, through the crowds, to the centre of the stadium.

Since then, God has faithfully guided me along my life's journey through good times and bad, answering my questions along the way.

Greg has continued in his faith journey over the years and uses his unique abilities and expertise to support others to fulfil their calling.

The insecurities in our lives surface in many ways and at unexpected times.

When I was working as a form tutor, I was responsible for a group of boys aged 12 to 14. You get to know a lot about the boys as you meet with them daily and observe them in class and the playground. It did not take long to recognise that there was a pecking order. There were two boys who bullied two of the other students, whom they sensed were weak and vulnerable. The bullying was mostly verbal but, of course, it still hurt.

As was usual for that particular school, we took the boys on an annual school camp for five days, and something very interesting unfolded the day we went abseiling. The two boys who were being bullied took up the abseiling challenge very positively, and one asked to do it again immediately. But the two who bullied them? They refused to abseil. Nothing could convince them to take hold of the rope and go over the edge. What was going on there?

We all have our ways of managing our insecurities. It wasn't that these two bullies were just bad people, but they looked for other students whom they could compare themselves to. By trying to put other boys down, they hoped to feel better about themselves. This bullying technique was what made the boys feel adequate, until the abseiling test came. As the saying goes, hurt people hurt people. Bullies are usually very insecure people, and the insecurities of these two boys were exposed for all their schoolmates to see. And all of this had unfolded as a result of self-comparison, which is invariably toxic.

'I felt very lonely and isolated.'

Comparing ourselves with others is a common way of establishing our self-worth. Greg chose another path – withdrawal. The consequence of his choice was overwhelming loneliness. He chose to head for safety when his deep desire was to relate and belong.

Let's understand that there is a big difference between being alone and being lonely. Sometimes being alone is a very welcome experience. We are free to do and be whatever we please. We do not have to consider others at that time. For many of us, 'alone time' can be an oasis in the bustle and stress of life.

Loneliness is not at all like that. We can feel lonely when we are alone, or we can feel lonely in a large crowd. Loneliness is a state of mind.

In our modern world, we don't often consider loneliness. There are so many distractions with which we can fill our hours and minutes. Music is at our fingertips 24/7. Social media and mobile technology keep us relentlessly up-to-date with the movements and activities of everyone we know. When we are not at work, or parenting or being educated, we have an endless arsenal of digital entertainment available to cram any remaining time in our day with distraction. Life can feel intensely busy, yet loneliness is everywhere. Unlike many other cultures, the Western world seems to have lost much of its sense of community; of needing each other; of being mutually dependent.

We need to feel we have a genuine purpose and place in our world. We need people close.

'I desperately wanted to go out on Friday nights – anywhere! – but sat alone at home.'

Greg recognised a deep longing to belong, but was hindered by powerful doubts concerning his own social adequacy. He faced the dilemma of wanting to take the risk but at the same time fearing what he believed would be inevitable rejection. Even the best people are not 100% reliable, trustworthy, or always accepting of us. It was his desperate loneliness, plus the timely invitation from his Christian friends, which led Greg on the journey of discovering God for himself.

I would suggest that our need for relationship with people is paralleled by our deep need for relationship with God. Security, significance and self-worth reside ultimately in God. When our deep need for a secure relationship surfaces it may be very painful – a yearning for something we cannot identify or explain with words. It is interesting that as Greg began to reach out and trust people, he also embarked on a journey to know and trust God.

> 'I had so many unanswered questions about the meaning of life and my existence... There were thousands of questions spinning in my young mind, all demanding answers.'

Greg started to find some of those answers when he became part of a community. He found a group of people that he trusted, and their company provided the fun and companionship he had desired for so long.

He began to develop the relationships he had wanted all his life. Surprisingly for Greg, this was not only with other people, but also with God Himself.

04

Created for relationship

'My faith now means everything to me. I was confused for the first 15 years of my life, not seeing any meaning to words or rules, but I ended up in a love affair with my creator, and have been now for more than 17 years.'

Hannah

How has the environment in which you grew up shaped your view of yourself and influenced your wellbeing or pain?

As we explored in the last chapter, we are relational beings, and need community with other people and with our creator. Greg's journey towards faith was birthed out of a sense of inner inadequacy and longing, as a result of the loneliness and marginalisation he felt. Hannah's search for God arose out of the disaster of a dysfunctional and damaging home life. As she grew up and became more aware of the relational struggles between her parents, Hannah tried to do what many hurting children do – she tried to be the answer to her family's problems.

'My search for meaning in life began with the sense as a child that my world was broken, and that I was not enough to make the people I loved happy.'

Of course, there was no way Hannah could address the needs of her parents, but as a result, she felt like a failure. Equally painful to her was the growing discovery that she was unable to mend the gaping emotional wound in her own life, or satisfy her unmet longings for self-worth and significance. This was part her life 'baggage' that she carried into her teenage years.

No family is perfect, but how much worse is it when, as children, we are terrified and emotionally damaged by living in an environment of anger, fighting and unpredictable behaviour from the nurturing figures in our lives? Hannah's experiences show how we can sometimes struggle to see beyond the challenges of daily emotional survival. Our view of life and the future can become distorted.

Hannah

From as far back as I can remember, I was always torn between seeing the Bible as a rulebook, and on the other hand seeing it as a means to a relationship with my creator. I didn't know how to think of God or the pain I experienced in the circumstances of my life. I was filled with confusion.

My search for meaning in life began with the sense as a child that my world was broken, and that I was not enough to make the people I loved happy. I felt so much pain seeing the war inside those who cared for me. I was particularly troubled by seeing the secret life of my father, who was lost in his addictions.

Things started to change when I met a girl at school who attended a warm and lively church, where people seemed to really believe in the things they were singing about. She was someone I saw freedom in – and I didn't like her! She seemed comfortable showing her emotions in every situation, and she was accepting of who she was... again, I definitely did not like that.

Having kept a heavy secret from a young age, I felt that I was bleeding emotionally and couldn't handle life anymore. I was in my year ten music class at school, crying on the inside, when this girl asked me if I wanted to visit her youth group. I would never have wanted to before that point in time, but she gently asked me,

'What do you have to lose?' So when I walked into that church and heard the expression of God's love so freely shown, I knew strangely that I was safe. It truly felt like home – and I cried for the first time in a very long while.

I knew that I had to hand over the pain and the heaviness of what I had been carrying for so long. It was hard to let go, and I cried all the harder when I realised that. But I was no longer alone, and let go of my secret within the caring pastoral counselling environment that was provided for me.

I felt that the Church was given to me that night as a gift from God to lift off the weights I was carrying. The Church was now here, and was not going anywhere. It would lead me, teach me and guide me on my new journey of giving God the responsibility of caring for my every need. I don't have to do it myself anymore. God has put back together the pieces of my heart.

My faith now means everything to me. I was confused for the first 15 years of my life, not seeing any meaning to words or rules, but I ended up in a love affair with my creator, and have been now for more than 17 years. As I move forward with my life, my struggle is to continually remember that God is never-ending. There is more of Him I have yet to experience or understand. He reminds me of this constantly, through every new trial and every unwelcome heartbreak, as I search for Him each time and see a new quality of love from Him that I had not seen before. I am constantly challenged to continue to make the choice to look for Him.

Our relationships contribute in a number of important ways to our early lives and through into our later years. Warm relationships provide us with a sense of acceptance and belonging. They stimulate the development of our security, significance, and self-worth. Relationships provide a context in which we may have the courage to own our failures and to dream our dreams. But when our closest relationships are as flawed as Hannah's, what then?

In my years as a counsellor, I have observed that people who grow up in highly dysfunctional contexts struggle with issues such as their own identity, and the ability to form trusting relationships. They carry many painful memories and a great deal of emotional baggage. Nevertheless, there is something deep within us that cries out for someone to understand us and to know us: accepting us unconditionally, even when they know the worst of our history. We all carry a 'love hunger', but we are ingenious at finding ways to distract ourselves in an effort to satisfy or disguise it. Attempting to satisfy our need for love with an inferior substitute (such as sex) can leave us feeling emptier. We want warmth, affection, safety and security, and unconditional acceptance – an incredibly high mandate for humans to fulfil. As parents, we rarely do it justice. Marriages creak and crack under the strain of pressure and apparent failure. As human beings, we are not enough for each other. We need more.

Hannah carried her pain and confusion until she confronted her creator. She found He was only too ready to accept her as she was, emotionally exhausted and confused about her life in general. As she began to build a relationship with Him, she found the courage to release her pain from the past and move on towards discovering her true identity. Emotional healing began.

Perhaps as you have read Hannah's story you identify with much of it yourself. Perhaps you know others who have followed a similar life path. But let me assure you, taking time out – for this critical search for meaning, for purpose, for God – will not be wasted time.

05

A different view of God

'Despite all the hard times I went through, God never gave up on me, and when I couldn't go on, He carried me.'

Anne

Whatever their belief system, most people have a view of God; an idea of what He is like – even if they don't believe He's real. To some, the image of a bearded, cloud-riding Zeus might spring to mind. For others, a fistful of lightning bolts and a booming voice of anger and judgment. Whatever our ideas, it's probable that most people don't imagine God to be joyful and loving. Consider many of the famous artworks depicting Jesus. How often is He smiling?

Theologian A.W. Tozer said, 'What comes into our minds when we think about God is the most important thing about us.'* There might be many reasons why we don't automatically picture a God of love, but in the Bible, Jesus describes God as *the* God of love. Take a moment now to reflect on your own ideas about God, and where they might have come from.

Anne endured physical, emotional and psychological abuse in her childhood home, and the consequences shaped her for many decades of her life. Few, if any, of Anne's early experiences, right up until her failed marriage, would have contributed to the development of a healthy sense of self-image, security or self-worth, despite the fact that she is a caring woman of high intellect and with many creative skills.

One of Anne's great challenges has been dismantling her view of God and replacing it with one more in keeping with the Bible. After all, who wants to trust a 'god' who is watching and recording every failure and checking whether we measure up to His standards, to see if we deserve to scrape our way into heaven? That kind of 'god' is very unattractive, yet so many people appear to believe that is what God is like. Douglas Schoeninger wrote: 'If you image a hostile God, don't open up to that god. That god is not only not valid, but that god is not anyone to whom to entrust yourself. Don't entrust yourself to that person.'**

Anne came to know that God is accepting and caring, and not the judgmental and distant deity she had pictured for much of her life. Here is her story.

Anne

I was the only girl of five children in my family, which you might think would be celebrated – but instead I was repeatedly told that it was a shame that I wasn't a boy, because boys were 'so much better than girls'. I was raised in a very old-fashioned, strict, and often abusive home. I felt completely unloved and worthless.

As a child I went to church and Sunday school, but it was never a family experience. I was sent rather than invited or accompanied, and for many years I lived under condemnation – especially from my family, but also from my misunderstanding at the time who God was. I was always striving to measure up, but inevitably falling short of the expectations that were placed upon me.

Growing up in such a controlling and abusive environment, I struggled to break free – only to leave one destructive situation and marry into another. Within days of being married I felt that I had made the biggest mistake of my life, but though I considered my marriage a complete failure, God blessed me with two beautiful daughters, who gave me the strength to carry on. I had so wanted a little girl of my own to love and cherish, and God blessed me with two. He always gives us more than we ask for or expect.

Despite all the hard times I went through, God never gave up on me, and when I couldn't go on, He carried me. He enabled me to be a mum who did not crush my daughters' dreams, but who encouraged them. He allowed me to break the patterns of physical, sexual and emotional abuse that were so present in my upbringing, and to love my girls completely and unconditionally.

Even when my marriage ended and I found myself as a single mum of two young children, God provided for me and my girls. He kept showing me that I had a future and a hope, just as He promises in Jeremiah 29:11. He made it possible for me to go to university and re-educate myself for a better future. He then provided me with a good job, and He has blessed me with two beautiful granddaughters.

Over the years I've faced many challenges with my health, my psychological wellbeing and my sense of security, but God has been with me all the way. It's a miracle that I am alive today. But my biggest breakthrough came when I found a church.

I have always been part of a church, but never really felt connected – as though I was on the outside looking in. I knew and loved Jesus, but always felt there was something missing; still a little bit disconnected. I travelled the world trying to find the missing pieces, and in September 2012, I returned to Australia after living for a time in the UK. While staying with one of my daughters, I went along to her church.

I was immediately made to feel so welcome! That same week, the church connected me with one of their 'life groups' – a smaller group that met weekly in someone's home, where we could get to know each other better, pray together, and chat about things that really matter. I was so welcomed and loved, and I truly felt that I had come home.

I had always had the head knowledge that God created and loved me, but now it's in my heart. I am His precious daughter and He loves me no matter what. My future looks bright, my girls are both planted into church, and I know that God has fantastic things in store for me. The best truly is yet to come.

'Over the years I've faced many challenges with my health, my psychological wellbeing and my sense of security, but God has been with me all the way. It's a miracle that I am alive today.'

No matter how ideal or undesirable our upbringing was, we face the inevitable trials of life. From life's early days, Hannah and Anne both suffered the daily experience of emotional and physical pain in an environment of insecurity and abuse. For Anne, it was her growing confidence in God's presence and love in the midst of various traumatic experiences over the decades of her life that helped her to survive.

Yet even for those of us who have had a more secure

childhood, life throws up the unexpected and often emotionally painful experiences: unexpected, unwelcome events that come out of nowhere and turn our world upside down.

I experienced something like this when on holiday with my family, aged 17. My two brothers and I were reading in the holiday cottage, and my parents had gone to the nearby bus stop, as Dad had to return to work the next day. It wasn't long before we heard a tremendous collision of vehicles outside and, as young boys do, we ran out to see what had happened. Two vehicles were at the intersection, one on its roof. To my horror, my eyes were drawn to my mum lying in the middle of the road, with blood on her clothes. I was so traumatised by the sight that I did not think to look for my dad. He was lying in the grass beside the road. He had taken the full impact of the collision, as one vehicle had rolled on him.

I travelled with my parents in the ambulance to the nearby major hospital, where Mum was admitted. (That trip in the ambulance was the last time my parents were to be together.) Because my father's injuries were so serious, the ambulance took him to another city with even more resources.

Being the eldest son, I travelled in the ambulance with him. We were a Christian family, and over the next few days I began to make deals with God about what I would do for Him if my dad lived. But within a few days he died from complications connected to his injuries.

Somewhat surprisingly, I did not lose my faith. But my understanding of God and His ways of working took a major hit. My neat and tidy views of God were no longer neat and tidy. Things I had been sure of were suddenly very confusing.

Our family was totally rearranged. My mother was in hospital for months, recovering from her injuries, so she could not work. One of my brothers had to get a job, rather than pursue his dream of going to university. In a way, I became the head of the family. While my youngest brother continued his schooling, life would never be the same for our family.

In the whirlpool of emotions that I experienced as I grieved, I had a deep certainty that God was somehow still there. While questions and confusion swirled around in my head, still there was a deep sense of God's peace and presence. How could that be?

In the years that followed our family tragedy, I witnessed God begin to fulfil His plans for us and in us (my brothers and me). We saw our mother restored to a functional level of health. We still don't understand why the accident occurred or why God did not stop it, but we have all grown in confidence that even the worst that life throws at us does not take Him by surprise. We watched as God surrounded us with people who helped us through those tough times: people who cared for us and gave us the support we needed.

Life-changing experiences can occur in an instant, or they may build up over many years. They don't always involve death. The possibilities for trouble appear to be endless. Yet it is often in these seasons of distress that we see things more clearly. We come to accept that we don't have the wisdom or power to overcome everything in our own strength. Our hearts may cry out for the intervention of God, even if we are unsure whether He exists.

In 1789, Benjamin Franklin famously said, 'In this world nothing can be said to be certain, except death and taxes.' Yet the death of someone close can shake us to the core. No amount of education, psychological awareness, worldly riches or success, pleasure or ability can guard us from the impact. Events such as these can easily destroy one's faith in God. Perhaps this has been your experience in the past.

There was a funeral service that took place at a crematorium. A man had lost his wife. As those who attended streamed out of the chapel, the bereaved husband and a few of his friends gathered together in a rough circle. None of the widower's friends knew what to say to him. Feet shuffled in discomfort – men wanting to support their friend, but uncertain of how to do it. After a time, someone had the courage to ask him, 'Are you OK?' 'Yes, I'm OK,' he said. 'What are we doing tonight?'

Some things in our lives can be too emotionally painful to face head on. The bereaved husband chose to push his emotions down and act tough, as though the loss of his wife was now history and he was ready to move on. But we humans are not wired like that. Buried emotions are never buried dead. They are always buried alive. Men particularly can find it very difficult to express and to talk about their feelings, but the same applies to women as well. We fear that admitting personal struggle and pain might be seen as a sign of weakness or inadequacy. In reality, healing begins when we acknowledge our pain with someone we trust.

Our response to the major events of our lives is rarely neutral. We will be pushed one way or the other. We may become depressed, or we may become more determined.

We may become sad, or we may become angry. We can grow through trials or be crushed by them. We may seek God for support or we may rail against Him for what He has allowed to happen.

Through her many physical struggles, Anne clung to her faith in God. And her faith grew stronger as she outgrew her childhood views and became confident that He would stand with her through all that she was facing. She is still the same today – I know her well.

*A.W. Tozer, *The Knowledge of the Holy* (San Francisco, CA, USA: HarperOne, 1978)

**Douglas Schoeninger et al., *Christian Anthropology: The nature of the human person, human brokenness and healing* (McLean, VA, USA: Association of Christian Therapists, 2009)

06

Open to ideas

'Are you tired? Worn out? Burned out on religion? Come to me. Get away with me and you'll recover your life. I'll show you how to take a real rest. Walk with me and work with me–watch how I do it. Learn the unforced rhythms of grace. I won't lay anything heavy or ill-fitting on you. Keep company with me and you'll learn to live freely and lightly.'

Jesus Christ, Matthew 11:28–30 (*The Message*)

You may have noticed that each story has a spiritual search woven into the individual's history. Of course, the word 'spiritual' has a range of meanings these days, but the idea points to something that is at the centre of our human identity but difficult to explain. Some Christians would say that it is like a 'God hunger'. How would you describe it?

Daniel

I was born into something of a career dynasty that was at odds with the Church. (Some church-going people have certainly let me know this in various ways over the years, although I never saw my activities and career that way.) My family were artists, through and through.

I spent my afternoons training in performing arts at my mother's school, where my brother and sister taught me as well. My father was often away performing and providing for us at home. It was a great upbringing – full of fun, discipline and physical activity. It was my training ground as an artist and became a safe place for me to discover my own artistry, which was less entertainment driven and more in the contemporary arts.

My parents raised me in a 'spiritual' household that didn't discriminate against other beliefs, although my family clearly had prejudices based on their own ideas, which at the time I knew little about. Because of this I was open to anything and everything. I explored my own spirituality through the confused channels my parents provided – there were horoscopes, but also Sunday school (which I was kicked out of for swearing at the teacher). There was one particular bedtime 'prayer' that terrifed me:

Now I lay me down to sleep,
I pray to God my soul to keep.
If I die before I wake,
I pray to God my soul to take.
God bless Mummy, Daddy...

I would name everyone who I wanted to be safe. The thought of dying in my sleep was very real to me as it was stated every night. Death was real, and I had my first experience of it when my favourite person in the world, my grandfather ('Pop') died, around the time I started school. Pop had lived with us in the past, and we were very close. He was my first friend – not a parent or sibling. This was so significant to me, and I spent hours under his chair while he watched *The Benny Hill Show*, laughing while his hearing aids whistled.

In the years that followed Pop's death, I would sometimes talk to him. I would lie out in the garden with my dog, and just talk away as if he could still hear me. I wondered how he possibly could.

I had lots of friends growing up, and because I was performing in lots of different media, I would maintain friendships with people all over the place. I wasn't alone and I don't think I was lonely, but I did often find myself thinking about deeper things. I had friends whose families had different spiritual or religious practices, so I'd try to learn a bit about them, or visit their church, and so on. I don't recall ever being opposed to any religion or spirituality. Because of my exposure to some violent horror films and news footage of the Iraq war, I was consciously aware of all the evil in the world, and wanted to try to make some sense of it. But horoscopes and other vague spiritual ideas weren't enough to explain it.

By the time I was in school year nine, I had already had a successful artistic career many performers would be grateful for. Still, I wasn't satisfied with who I was becoming. Nathan, someone I went to school with, was someone I admired as a friend, and we remained close friends into our early twenties. Nathan's dad was a pastor at the local Baptist church, and while they were clearly 'religious', they were a humble family, fun, relaxed, non-judgmental, honest, and very welcoming to anyone. I had never met anyone like them. I had seen families that were fun and welcoming, but never so open and lacking judgment of others. Nathan's family embodied the concept of grace, but I didn't understand it at the time, and it would be years before I really did.

Another person who influenced me was the senior pastor of the church I was attending. He always encouraged us not to take his word as gospel, but to read the Bible ourselves and make up our own minds. I was doing that, but as a result, was wrestling with some of the advice and beliefs that others in the church expected me to adopt. I was still forming my own understanding on a number of issues, and though I respect and value the opinions of others, some things were a real struggle for me.

My family didn't take to my decision to believe in

and follow Jesus too well, as they assumed that having someone who was self-righteous and judgmental around the house would create tensions. I had chosen a single way, when my family preferred many paths. I had to learn how to live my faith for myself while living at home. It raised a lot of questions between us all.

'Conviction' in my beliefs happened over a period of time, but I'm not sure about that word either. I believe that Jesus is God and present now in Spirit. These days, my understanding of salvation is changing. However, I can say that I believe we all make mistakes, and so having grace to be wrong, sit in a place of changing belief, and hold to a belief, is essential. I think it is also the source of any humility I may be grateful for. It also means I am suspicious of anyone who says this is the only way or the only truth, and everyone else has it wrong. I'm relying on Jesus to cover what I don't understand or what I get wrong.

I continue to struggle with contemporary church forms. From what I read in the Bible and Early Church history, and my own early Baptist church experience, it's about the people you journey with, and your own journey, with Jesus. A pastor is there to help you grow and continue your journey.

A personal struggle, which I would say is common to the human condition, is learning to love and be loved. Being vulnerable with others is something I struggle with. I seem like an open person but I'm not. I'm just more comfortable about discussing or sharing information about myself that I know is common to everyone. But I do find it easy to be vulnerable with God. I think that's because I firmly believe grace and mercy trump judgment. I think that's where marriage is excellent. If it's safe, mutual, and loving, then one could learn to be truly known by another human without judgment. That too is a long-term journey.

I love the title of Eugene Peterson's book, *A Long Obedience in the Same Direction*. That title alone speaks of the four fundamental pillars in my life: God, wife, children and friends. Long-term relationships, consistently choosing to journey with each other. That is the path to intimacy. Easy to have with God, but often difficult to have with humans.

'I was open to anything and everything. I explored my own spirituality through the confused channels my parents provided'

During the Second World War, many occupied towns and villages in parts of Europe pulled down their signs to confuse the enemy. It was a good strategy. Daniel's parents effectively did the same for him. He was encouraged to explore whatever form of spirituality appealed to him at the time. While his parents were content with a degree of blurriness in their spiritual beliefs, Daniel began to search for something more concrete to fix his life upon. It appears that the death of his grandfather had something to do with this decision. The fear of death (rooted in his frightening night prayer) added incentive to his search.

Every person's spiritual journey, whether towards God or away from God, is different. Like Daniel, we can choose to follow those we respect and trust, or we can find our own way. As Daniel put it, 'I had chosen a single way, when my family preferred many paths.' It's easy to admire Daniel for finding his way forward in the confusing world of 'anything goes' spirituality. People who are further along in their journey with God can be very encouraging and supportive. The key people Daniel met were a critical factor in his journey towards finding the creator God for himself.

Reading Daniel's story, I wonder: why do we humans look for some higher power? Why do so many of us recognise that we face compelling questions that we cannot answer, and challenging situations that we are inadequate to meet or control?

A deep, serious search for God is rarely undertaken accidentally. Something or someone usually takes hold of our attention and motivates us to consider whether there is a God and, if so, what are His characteristics? To fully grasp the idea of an infinite, supremely wise, powerful and creative being is beyond the thinking capacity of our finite minds. Nevertheless, we search to give our existence a context, and to ascribe meaning to our lives. Sometimes the reality of our mortality raises the question: is this all there is?

Asking that simple question can be the start of a slow but steady journey towards answers. When my wife and I were living in South-East Tasmania many years ago, I was teaching religious education classes for a few weeks in a regional school. Driving back one afternoon, I noticed a young man hitch-hiking ahead of me. My usual behaviour would be to drive on without stopping on the grounds of safety, but on this occasion, on impulse, I pulled over. Once he settled into the car, he asked me where I had come from and what I had been doing. I told him about my religious education classes.

He replied, 'You're a Christian, are you? How do you even know there *is* a God?' He was somewhat puzzled with my reply: 'You're a university student, are you?'

'How did you know that?' he asked.

With a smile I replied, 'University students often ask questions like that.'

As we talked, I discovered he was indeed a student of biology at the University of Queensland. We seemed to 'click', and we had an interesting exchange of ideas and questions. As we drove closer to my home, I invited him in for a coffee and we talked some more. Interestingly, he mentioned that on his travels around Australia, he had encountered a number of other Christians, and had had enjoyable and thoughtful discussions with them.

Sometime later, he decided it was time to continue on his journey. At the door, ready to leave, he paused and asked a final question with a smile: 'For me to become a Christian, do you think it will be enough for me to be curious, or will I need to be desperate?'

I replied, 'I think you will have to be desperate.'

He smiled back and said, 'I agree.' He walked from the door towards the road and left, looking for another car to pick him up. I never saw him again, but I do wonder whom he has since met to continue his discussions about God.

Daniel started his spiritual journey in the wide-open

expanses of his parents' spirituality, where anything was up for consideration. Intellectual curiosity will get us so far in our search for God. It is very useful to know what the Bible says about God the Father, His Son Jesus Christ, and the Holy Spirit. However, some biblical experts have never had an encounter that brought them into relationship with their creator. Years ago, I heard something said by a speaker at a conference that really stuck in my mind. It went something like this: 'A brilliant, blind physicist may be able to describe all the physical qualities of the light spectrum, but a simple, uneducated washerwoman who stares in awe at a beautiful sunset understands light and beauty much better.' I believe it is the same for us in our search for God. Encounter beats information any day.

*Eugene Peterson, *A Long Obedience in the Same Direction: Discipleship in an Instant Society* (Westmont, IL, USA: Intervarsity Press, 2000)

07

Desperately seeking love

'Love is patient, love is kind. It does not envy, it does not boast, it is not proud. It does not dishonour others, it is not self-seeking, it is not easily angered, it keeps no record of wrongs. Love does not delight in evil but rejoices with the truth. It always protects, always trusts, always hopes, always perseveres. Love never fails.'

1 Corinthians 13:4–8

A key distinguishing feature of what makes the human race unique is our quest for love. Grace's story is a very common tale of effort and seemingly dead ends as she relentlessly sought after love through different people and through various experiences.

We most often look to other human beings to complete us – but that will never be enough. But why do we need love? What does that say about us as created individuals?

Grace

My earliest memory is of my father being taken away on a stretcher by two ambulance men – I never saw him again. I was just three and a half years old. He had suffered a major brain haemorrhage and died a few days later. As was usual in those days, I didn't go to his funeral, as children simply didn't attend funerals then. My mum was a strong lady and I don't remember ever seeing her cry, even when she told me that my father wasn't coming home. She simply explained that it was 'just us now', and we needed to be strong, because 'big girls don't cry'. Those words have echoed through my life over the years.

I can't say that my childhood was unhappy – precisely the opposite, in fact. I had plenty of friends and I loved school. Mum remarried when I was eight to the man I now call Dad (and to whom I am still very close).

Faith simply wasn't mentioned in our household. My dad had absolutely no interest in it, and my mum was closed to it to the extent of being quite anti-God.

That said, when my friend asked if I wanted to go to the local Baptist church's 'Holiday Bible Club' with her and I subsequently started to go to church on a weekly basis, my parents didn't object. But nor did they ever come with me.

As a teenager, I joined the church youth group. In the 1970s, 'God is love' is what was taught at church. I understood the concept of a loving God who was my heavenly Father, but He seemed to remain quite distant from me (mirroring my own experience of loss and abandonment through the death of my father).

Like most teenagers, I was seeking to discover who I was and whether I was worthy of being loved. I was incredibly good at putting on a front of self-confidence, but inside I was a damaged, emotionally vulnerable young girl, who was desperately seeking to fill the gap left by the loss of her father through the admiration and approval of others – especially boys. I fell into sexual relationships at a very young age, seeking love in all the wrong places.

At age 14 I was drinking, self-harming, and dating boys a lot older than myself. But I was still attending church, and had a profound experience at the baptism of someone I knew. (I now realise that I was touched by the Holy Spirit, but at that stage I only knew that something had happened to me.) I went home in floods of tears. When I tried to explain what I had experienced to my mum she dismissed it, and made me feel silly for even mentioning it. My church attendance dwindled after that, and I finally stopped going altogether shortly before my fifteenth birthday. I felt I was being a hypocrite as I was getting drunk with my friends on a Saturday night, and then going to church the following morning. I would always say that I believed in God and would certainly pray, especially during difficult times, but that was as far as it went for me.

I had wanted to join the police since the age of 12, but at the age of 18 I wasn't quite tall enough (I was just one centimetre too short). The recruiting sergeant made a throw-away comment that the police would only allow people to join below the height limit in 'exceptional circumstances'. I asked what these were, and he mentioned service in the armed forces. On that basis, I decided to apply for the Army.

I joined the Army at the age of 19 and, after a very tough and intensive period of training, emerged as a Lance Corporal in the Royal Military Police. After a short period in England, I applied to serve in Northern Ireland. It was there that I met and married my first husband. I was just 21. It was at that stage that my mum fell ill, but she hid from me just how bad it was. What I was told was a minor operation on her lung turned out to be extensive treatment for lung cancer. Further treatment meant she couldn't travel to Northern Ireland for my wedding, but she wouldn't hear of me moving it. I was devastated, but I still had my dad with me, who proudly walked me down the aisle.

On the surface things looked like they were going OK. I was successful in my career, but the marriage was a huge mistake. I was desperately seeking love and someone to 'complete me' – an impossible task for any person – and he was emotionally distant. We had very different expectations from our marriage. I certainly was not the wife that he needed and, as his drinking got more out of control, the marriage dissolved into violence. I had no one to turn to and nowhere to go. Life was at an all-time low, but I kept the mask in place at work, hid the bruises, and simply got on with things.

Big girls don't cry.

Then my mum died. I was distraught. She was my rock, my strong right arm, my supporter, the person who loved me most – I was left feeling like a rudderless ship. My mum's words from my childhood about being strong and not crying also came flooding back to me, and so I went home to help my dad and be strong for him.

Life was never the same for me afterwards, and although my first husband tried to support me as I grieved, he really didn't have the emotional capacity to do so. Things within our marriage went from bad to worse, eventually coming to a head with him trying to strangle me. Our marriage never recovered. After I confronted him about his alcoholism, he went AWOL (Absent Without Leave). We never saw each other again and we divorced some five years later.

At the age of 29, I left the Army and I finally achieved my goal of joining the police. After I finished my initial police training, I purchased and then moved into my own flat. I had been on my own for quite some time and I was lonely. It was then that people from a local church came knocking at my door and invited me to a Start course (similar to the Alpha course), and I agreed. The church I started going to was very different from my earlier experience of church, as it met in a school and the sung worship was in a contemporary style that I wasn't used to. But it was home.

The course was great – I found answers to many of my questions, and started to understand that Jesus really loved me. I finally came to the point of realising that if God truly existed then I needed to respond to Him. Before falling asleep one night I said, 'God, if You truly exist, please prove it to me.' The next day, I picked up a newspaper. Imagine my amazement when I turned to the international news section and saw a picture of my ex-husband there. I understood that this was God answering my question – He exists! That evening, when I got home, I gave my life to God. I was immediately able to forgive my ex-husband. I prayed for him and I no longer experienced any of the nightmares or fears that had become my norm since our marriage. God is so good!

Over time I met a man called Grant, who also came to know Jesus and got baptised. We got married the year after that, and have now had more than 20 very happy years together.

As I have walked with God over the years, I have met many amazing people who have really spoken into my life, shared my journey, helped bear my burdens, encouraged me and, where necessary, given me a well-deserved spiritual talking-to.

God never abandoned me – He waited so patiently for me to come to Him. He stood with me throughout all of my years of hurt and disappointment, waiting until I was ready and able to receive His fatherly love. In truth, I was never alone! Over the years, I have received significant emotional healing from God, especially in the areas of abandonment and loss. I want to continue walking with Him for as long as I live.

Early loss of a significant adult (such as a parent or carer) is emotionally wounding. The grieving process – and the healing of emotional wounds caused by loss – can be hindered by adults who tell a bereaved child to take control of their emotions.

'Big girls don't cry.'

Sadly, this all too common view goes against our characteristics as emotional beings.

My first year as a newly qualified teacher was spent feeling totally unprepared and in charge of a composite Year 3–4 class with a wide range of student abilities and needs. I have many warm memories from that time, but also some sad ones. There is one experience I will never forget. The eight-year-olds in my class were playing softball in the school playground. The ball was soft, but the bat was solid aluminium. One of the young boys was the backstop, proudly wearing his catcher's glove. As I watched, one of the batters gave a lusty back swing that cracked squarely on the catcher's nose. I expected him to fall to the ground, screaming with pain, but to my amazement he merely shook his head, and with tears in his eyes, he took his place again.

Big boys don't cry. Beaten boys don't cry either.

His emotions were well under control and deeply buried. I wondered what he'd been through to help him master such a level of emotional control at such a young age. I also wondered how this attitude would affect his adult life.

Painful emotions can be pushed down (suppressed), but they are always buried 'alive', as we noted previously. They will affect us, often in surprising and unexpected ways. Sometimes they surface when we least expect it. How many painful feelings can bubble up inside us; grief, loss, rejection, loneliness, anxiety, guilt, shame, anger, abandonment, hopelessness and so on.

'Over the years, I have received significant emotional healing from God, especially in the areas of abandonment and loss.'

Part of Grace's journey towards God was by finding a release from her childhood emotional pain. Her emotions had been 'buried alive' for many years. As she says: 'I was a damaged, emotionally vulnerable young girl, who was desperately seeking to fill the gap left by the loss of her father'. She found in God a safe place to be open about her pain and to release it to the *someone* who loves her unchangingly, knows her intimately and accepts her completely, just as she is.

If you have been searching for solid, unconditional love or a release from deep emotional pain, Grace's path is worth considering. To her surprise, she discovered that God is true love.

08

Finding 'Father'

'You will seek me and find me when you seek me with all your heart.'

Jeremiah 29:13

Over the past century or so, the Western world has been deconstructing its Christian roots and rejecting the religious foundation that it was built upon over many centuries. In the process many have abandoned the quest for God. Others would say that God is irrelevant in the contemporary world. Many would go further still and be openly hostile to the idea of God, and consider all religions as a route to control, bondage and oppression. Sadly, history provides them with many concrete examples of this occurring.

Matt's story begins with this type of hostile attitude, which makes his journey quite intriguing and challenging.

Matt

I grew up in an entirely non-Christian family. In my early childhood we lived in a fairly working class area, and I remember having friends from families of several different cultures, races and religious backgrounds. Most families I knew seemed to go to church only once or twice a year on 'special occasions', but otherwise didn't ever talk about having a faith of any kind. Looking back, it's fairly clear that they just went to church on Christmas Day (and sometimes on Easter Sunday too) as that was 'the thing to do' at that time of year, rather than out of any real religious belief.

My family didn't even go to church at Christmas or Easter. It's not that we were particularly against religion – I just don't think my family saw it as relevant to their lives. To this day I don't think my parents have ever really thought about 'the meaning of life' beyond trying to make ends meet and to stay healthy and happy. I would imagine that, like most English families with no other religious belief at that time, they would have ticked 'Christian – Church of England' on the census form, when 'agnostic' or 'never really thought about it' would probably be a better description.

As a teenager I found myself asking deeper questions, but often ended up arguing against Christians and thinking of them as ignorant and hypocritical. I became a staunch atheist and saw Christianity (and religion in general) as the 'opium of the masses', designed by those in power to control the feeble-minded. I started researching several religions as a sort of academic exercise (for me, everything was about intellect – the human mind was the only god to be worshipped). During a debate with a very gracious Christian college friend, I was invited to come and see church for myself, so I went along primarily to get ammunition to use against Christians in arguments. I thought that if there's no God, then there are no consequences to our actions, so it wouldn't matter if I sat in church for a bit to see what made these crazy Christians turn up every Sunday.

I expected it to be a bunch of old people sitting in a cold, dark room, talking about flower arranging, or a group of wild-haired hippies lighting candles and chanting mindlessly. Thankfully, it wasn't anything like that at all. It made me think that I should look into this whole Christianity thing a bit more closely, and not wanting to get a one-sided view, I decided to look into each of the world's major religions for comparison. I found that the more I learnt about Christianity, the more it started to make sense. 'Treat others how you'd want to be treated' sounded pretty good to me as a personal philosophy and as a logical solution to society's greatest needs.

I didn't suddenly become a Christian overnight. It was (and to some extent, still is) a gradual process. I wanted to test Christianity and God for historical evidence and see whether it all stood up to logic and reasoning. I first accepted God in my mind as more of an abstract theory, and only later accepted Him into my life on a relational level. This led to some months, even years, of falling back into my old ways and, quite frankly, not acting out my new-found beliefs or behaving in a particularly 'Christian' manner.

Eventually it did all click, and I had a sort of revelation – what Christians sometimes call an 'in-dwelling of the Spirit'. This was when I realised that God isn't some far away, impersonal being, but a loving Father who cares for all of us and wants to get to know us, and for us to get to know Him.

This is a continuing journey for me – there's always something new to discover. I like being part of a community of people trying to figure it all out together and helping each other along. Even though life won't always be a walk in the park, I now know that the ups and downs are much easier to handle with God by my side and fellow Christians around me.

Through Matt's journey to faith, he seems to identify a number of steps along the way.

1. He had no engagement with church, and thought religion to be irrelevant.
2. He had deeper questions, but would end up arguing against Christians, whom he thought to be ignorant and hypocritical.
3. He decided he was a staunch atheist.
4. He still had questions, so started researching major world religions as an academic exercise, approaching his search intellectually, rather than spiritually.
5. During a debate with a Christian friend, he was invited to church. Out of curiosity, he accepted, on the basis that he could gain more ammunition for their debates.
6. He realised church was not what he expected.
7. The more he found out about Christianity – through friendship, research, and church attendance – the more it started to make sense to him.
8. He first accepted God as an abstract theory, and later accepted Him into his life on a relational level.

'God isn't some far away, impersonal being, but a loving Father who cares for all of us and wants to get to know us'

One of the commendable qualities that I observe in Matt is his willingness to remain open-minded, even though his views were strongly held. A closed mind blocks our ability to see things differently and, as a result, keeps us from understanding and accepting new ideas. As you think about your own life, can you identify any similarities to Matt's experiences? Can you say, like Matt, that you have strong opinions about God, but are willing to go on a journey of discovery?

A lot of people won't even enter a church unless invited to a wedding or funeral. I've met many people who've joked that if they did, they would 'catch fire' – or that some other divinely-ordained punishment would befall them – just for daring to set foot in God's house.

One example in particular comes to mind. It was a beautiful wedding in a church building. The young bride and groom looked elegant and very much in love. The wedding service was full of contemporary Christian music, and there was lots of happiness, with a good mix of formality and humour. As the guests were leaving the building, a woman who clearly did not attend church commented to me, 'I really enjoyed the music.'

I said to her, 'That's the kind of music we play on Sunday, and you are more than welcome to come.'

'I could never do that,' she said, 'if I did, the roof would fall in.' And she never did come back.

It's sad how many people assume they're not good enough to come into God's presence. Of course, in one sense, it is totally true. None of us are good enough. But there's another side to that story, and to understand it we have to look at the life of Jesus and how He described His heavenly Father in His teaching and stories.

The people who criticised Jesus the most were the religious leaders of the day. They were highly offended that He spent so much time with people that they considered to be sinners; down-and-outs; 'scum'; enemies. Their view was that God would have nothing to do with them because they did not measure up. On the other hand, Jesus seemed to enjoy meeting up with the prostitutes, beggars, the corrupt tax collectors, and those who came from other cultures – so much so that many of His miracles and some of the stories He told involved people just like that. He ruffled the feathers of the religious leaders, and through His incredible wisdom dismantled their arguments. Not a good way to make friends!

Like the woman at the wedding I went to, you may have felt that being in God's presence would be a threatening place to be. Or you may have said to yourself, 'I am not good enough for God to accept me.' Be encouraged by the words Jesus spoke to answer His religious critics: 'I have come to call not those who think they are righteous, but those who know they are sinners and need to repent' (Luke 5:32, NLT).

Before we give up on the idea of searching for God, it is important to realise that He has been searching for us, and waiting for us to respond to a relationship with Him. He is eager to connect with people who are aware of their faults, and aware that they need His forgiveness – people just like you and me.

Part Two: Welcome Home

09

Remembering where we belong

'But while he was still a long way off, his father saw him and was filled with compassion for him; he ran to his son, threw his arms round him and kissed him.'

Luke 15:20

In this section of the book, we look at another story – a very old story that helps to tie all the other stories together. It is a story told by Jesus the Messiah, a master teacher, who Christians believe is the Son of God. Jesus told this story to help the people who heard Him understand that the creator God, who Jesus claimed was His Father, is the best, most loving and forgiving Father anyone could hope to find.

This story has three parts that all paint a very different understanding of God compared to the common view of His time… and probably a different view from the one many of us have today.

As we have noted previously, the religious 'policemen' of Jesus' day were highly offended by the fact that He mixed with people they considered to be the religiously unclean – the lowlife types, the losers, the immoral, the unethical, and the socially undesirable – anyone who did not measure up to their standards. Jesus taught a fundamentally different view of God to theirs. His stories and ideas turned their views of God's attitude towards people upside down. Because of His radical ideas, these religious leaders found Jesus to be offensive and dangerous. Their views of God were rigid and merciless, and they themselves were extremely self-righteous.

Some of us may find the idea of God as a loving Father hard to grasp because of our poor experience of father figures in our own lives. Some of us may have had a strict religious church connection in our earlier years and, as a result, we have formed a totally unattractive image of God as distant, judgmental, harsh or very demanding – not at all pleased with our efforts at living life. Others may have been abandoned by their fathers; even abused. But if God truly is exactly as Jesus described Him in the story written below, then surely, it's life-changing news for all of us.

The Parable of the Lost Son

(Luke 15:11–32)

'Jesus continued: "There was a man who had two sons. The younger one said to his father, 'Father, give me my share of the estate.' So he divided his property between them.

"Not long after that, the younger son got together all he had, set off for a distant country and there squandered his wealth in wild living. After he had spent everything, there was a severe famine in that whole country, and he began to be in need. So he went and hired himself out to a citizen of that country, who sent him to his fields to feed pigs. He longed to fill his stomach with the pods that the pigs were eating, but no one gave him anything.

"When he came to his senses, he said, 'How many of my father's hired servants have food to spare, and here I am starving to death! I will set out and go back to my father and say to him: Father, I have sinned against heaven and against you. I am no longer worthy to be called your son; make me like one of your hired servants.' So he got up and went to his father.

"But while he was still a long way off, his father saw him and was filled with compassion for him; he ran to his son, threw his arms around him and kissed him.

"The son said to him, 'Father, I have sinned against heaven and against you. I am no longer worthy to be called your son.'

"But the father said to his servants, 'Quick! Bring the best robe and put it on him. Put a ring on his finger and sandals on his feet. Bring the fattened calf and kill it. Let's have a feast and celebrate. For this son of mine was dead and is alive again; he was lost and is found.' So they began to celebrate.

"Meanwhile, the elder son was in the field. When he came near the house, he heard music and dancing. So he called one of the servants and asked him what was going on. 'Your brother has come,' he replied, 'and your father has killed the fattened calf because he has him back safe and sound.'

"The elder brother became angry and refused to go in. So his father went out and pleaded with him. But he answered his father, 'Look! All these years I've been slaving for you and never disobeyed your orders. Yet you never gave me even a young goat so I could celebrate with my friends. But when this son of yours who has squandered your property with prostitutes comes home, you kill the fattened calf for him!'

"'My son,' the father said, 'you are always with me, and everything I have is yours. But we had to celebrate and be glad, because this brother of yours was dead and is alive again; he was lost and is found.'"

For many years I missed so much of the significance of this story, and misunderstood even more! If asked to do so, I would probably have retold this powerful story (or parable) in words something like this:

> *A rich property owner in a rural community had two sons. The younger became tired of life on the farm and asked for his part of his inheritance before his father died. The father, who loved his boys very much, agreed and divided his estate between his two boys. Not long after, the younger son sold what he could and moved away from the farm to live an extravagant life overseas.*
>
> *Eventually his money ran out, and there was a severe food crisis. He became so desperate he took the only work he could find – tending pigs. He had no friends and no food. Even the pig food looked good to him.*
>
> *He came to senses, and realising that his father's hired workers were in a much better place than he was, he thought of a plan to win his father's favour. His father saw him coming towards home and rushed to meet him, hugging and kissing him, filthy though he was. He was reinstated into the family and the father called for a huge celebration. The elder brother was so angry he refused to join in. The end.*

Yet if we really want to understand the power of this story, we need to dig into the culture in which it was told. What point was Jesus making with this story? A Middle-Eastern listener in the first century would have been shocked by the events in this narrative.

First, let's recognise the target audience and the context. We can identify this group of people at the beginning of Luke 15. Jesus' audience were the religious elite, who had complained because Jesus was spending time with people who were unacceptable to them, and who were on the fringes of the Jewish society. Unlike the religious leaders, they broke many of the religious and cultural laws of the day. They were social outcasts, at the bottom of society, yet Jesus accepted them and enjoyed their company and their meals. This parable (which means a story Jesus told) is part of Jesus' answer to the leaders' question about why He associated with people like this. The story contains a strong challenge to the religious leaders who were listening.

The father at the centre of the story clearly represented God the Father – and even Jesus Himself. This father in the parable is extremely wealthy with vast assets in property, herds and money. At his death, his estate would be shared proportionally between the two sons, with the eldest receiving the major part, as was the custom.

Taking too long to die

The first shocking part of the story for the listeners was the audacity of the younger son in asking for his inheritance *now*. In effect, he was inferring that his father was taking too long to die. Normally, in the Middle-Eastern culture of the day, the father – who had all authority – would have become outraged. He may have ordered his son to be whipped or even disinherited.

But not this father. He calmly agrees and divides his inheritance between *both* sons – everything. And within a short period of time, the younger son sells off what he can and takes all his inheritance to another country, abandoning his family and his history for the 'good life' he has been dreaming of.

Selling off the inheritance

This sale would have been another shocking part of the story to those listening. Among the younger son's assets would have been land. Land was passed down from generation to generation. It was not something that could simply be sold to anyone who would buy it. The local villagers would have been both amazed and appalled by this sale. It is improbable that any of them would have bought the land, so it would most likely have been sold to an outsider – perhaps someone not even of their culture or religion. The likely outcome of this insult to the father and to the villagers would have been a ceremony to cut off the wayward son from the village. He would never have been welcome to return. He would have been banned and shamed for his outrageous behaviour towards his father and the village.

In the meantime, the young man was spending extravagantly and enjoying his new life... until the money ran out. Unfortunately for him, at the same time, a devastating famine descended on the country. The economy crashed. The only job he could find was feeding pigs.

Let's remember that this story was told to respectable Jewish religious leaders, who would have had nothing to do with pigs. Pigs were seen as 'unclean' animals, so to associate with them in any way was a religious taboo

– repulsive, even. To make the impact of the story still stronger, the starving young man is looking at the pig food with envy. How low can you go?

Jesus neatly links the wretched young man with the very people He is accused of associating with. Both are rejected by society because of their lifestyle and behaviour. You can almost see the strong disapproval on the faces of those listening.

Welcome home

The young man may have been desperate and he may have been starving, but he comes up with a carefully crafted plan. First, he recognises that his father loved him in the past, and perhaps still does, despite his awful behaviour. The hired workers at the home property are well fed, so he decides that he will approach his dad and ask to become one of them. He plans to admit his failures to his father. It could work. He may find food and employment on the family property, if all goes well.

But in this story, the father is watching for the son. Clearly there is pain and longing in his heart. He wants reconciliation. Day after day, he looks out and does not see his son. And then, one day, he sees him in the distance. Immediately he begins to *run to him* and his servants follow, amazed at what they are seeing. Wealthy men don't run in the culture of that time and place. They don't show their legs by hitching up their robes in order to allow them to run. These are culturally shameful things to do. Yet the father does both these things out of love for his son. He is willing to pay any price, and overcome any embarrassment or shame for the love of this lost young man.

And then there is the matter of the village ban on the son's return. The father's approach is simple and effective. He interrupts his dirty and hungry son in the middle of his prepared speech. He throws his arms around him, pulls him close, hugs him and publicly kisses him. The young man is in tattered rags, covered with the smell and stains of the pigs he has been feeding, but his father is not put off by any of this. The hearers of the story would have cringed at the father's shameful actions. Why would he do this for someone who had been so offensive and rebellious?

To confirm that his son is welcomed back into the family, the father calls for the family robe and the ring of authority to be placed on him. The father calls for sandals for his son. Servants had bare feet. Sons did not.

Father and son are reunited completely, but at great personal cost to the father. The villagers dare not touch the returning son now. He has been welcomed home by the father.

Jesus is saying through this story that no matter how far away from God we are, or how low or dirty or shameful or lost we may feel, we are loved and we are welcomed back into God's family.

Nothing is spared from the celebration that follows the return of the son. His head must have been spinning as he thought of what was happening and the extravagant love and forgiveness of his father. The central reason for the party is the father's success in finding what was lost, what was precious to him. His lost son has been found and has been reunited into the family.

Two lost sons

It would be easy to think that the story is about the wayward son, and that the main point is that he came back home. But actually, it is the elder brother who holds the key to understanding this story. The religious leaders are being portrayed in the character and attitude of the elder brother. The story was actually all about *them*, rather than the boy who left home!

A closer look shows that both brothers had a very poor attitude to their father. Both wanted what he had, but placed little value on their relationship with him. The father, on the other hand, put his relationship with them as his top priority, whatever it cost.

The anger and the accusations of the elder brother that surfaced because of the 'welcome home' given to his disgraced younger brother were intended to mirror what the religious leaders were doing to the social and religious outcasts in their society. Like the elder brother, they believed they had earned something from God because of their good behaviour. In a very real sense, both brothers had lost their way – one at home and one in a foreign land.

The celebration is open to the elder brother too, but his response is anger and a stubborn refusal. Once again, the father takes the culturally shameful action of leaving his guests and pleading with his furious son, who accuses his father of neglect and favouritism. How humiliating that must have been!

Jesus portrays a radical view of God as Father. God was not at all like a Middle-Eastern family patriarch, and certainly not a despotic clan leader. Jesus Christ reveals the Father's attitude towards us through this story. He is compassionate, tender-hearted and relational.

One word that particularly resonates with me when I read this story concerns the father's attitude to the returning son: he had *compassion* on him. To me, this word embodies many qualities: love, understanding, forgiveness and unconditional acceptance. Jesus is telling us through this story that this is the attitude of our heavenly Father towards us, even when we are at our lowest and worst. How encouraging! How inviting!

The end of the story is carefully crafted. The invitation to join the celebration of the father is still open. How will the religious elite respond? We are not told. The story remained open-ended, just as it is for us today. We may identify more with the wayward son, or with the morally upright and well-behaved religious elder brother. Either way, we have the need and the opportunity to allow God the Father to find us, forgive us, give us a new beginning, and welcome us home into His family.

Finding our way home

Each of the brothers personifies a different way in which we can lose our relationship with God:

1. Living life based on our own desires and our personal rules, and finding that we can't make it work.

2. Being very 'religious'; trying to earn the favour of God by self-effort, doing more 'good' things than 'bad' things.

What both sons did not realise is that they were both lost and, in different ways, estranged from their father. Like these two brothers, we can so easily become lost and separated from our heavenly Father – who is the source of love, safety and hope for each one of us. The truth is, we may not even know that we are lost or that a better life is available to us. This was Emily's situation.

Emily's journey home

When writing this section I (Ron) was reminded of a unique encounter I had with a young woman. From having no interest in God or anything religious, she was catapulted into her own personal search. Because it was so unusual, I remember my meeting with her fairly clearly. It occurred something like this.

Emily was a nurse in her twenties, working in a retirement village. She appeared to be very confident and full of life. Then, something quite puzzling occurred. Her brother, who was at university, told her that he had become a Christian. This was the last thing Emily expected. Their family had not been churchgoers, and Emily had zero knowledge of the Bible or anything remotely 'Christian'. What did her brother mean? She worried that he had got caught up in some kind of cult.

It just so happened that at the same time as her brother broke his perplexing news to Emily, a retired matron, who once worked at that same nursing home as Emily did now, was on relief duty there. From talking with her, Emily discovered that the relief matron had been a Christian for many years.

When they were alone, Emily raised the issue of her brother.

'My brother is at university, and he phoned to say he has become a Christian,' she said. 'What does that mean? Has he been brainwashed by a bunch of weirdos?'

The matron suggested that Emily come and have a chat with me as I was the pastor of a nearby church at that time. Emily, never being one to dodge a challenge, decided to give it a try. She phoned me and arranged to meet me at the church building where I worked. When she arrived for the appointment, she was looking for a 'religious-looking person' like she had seen on TV, wearing robes and regalia and so on. As usual, I was casually dressed in jeans and a t-shirt, so she asked where she could find the pastor.

'I'm the person you are looking for,' I said with a grin.

'You don't look like a pastor,' she replied.

I chuckled at that. 'How can I help you?' I asked.

Emily didn't waste any time but, in her usual way, came straight to the point. 'My brother phoned and told me he's become a Christian at uni. What does that mean? My matron friend suggested I discuss my question with you. She seems to trust you.'

I began by briefly explaining the Bible teaching concerning God, creation, and who Jesus is. I explained that God created the world and everything it, and it was perfect in every way. Human beings chose to live their lives in their own wisdom and strength, but the result was disastrous, and only resulted in the ultimate betrayal of ourselves and of others, and a wrecked relationship with God. The cancer of 'sin' had found a way in, and was not only destroying our ability to live in the way we would want, but death was there at the end for everyone.

But that wasn't the end of the story. God sent His Son, Jesus, to bear the consequences of everything we've ever done wrong. When He died a cruel and unjust death on a Roman cross, He actually paid off the death sentence that every human deserves. His sacrifice bought us back for God. But death couldn't keep Jesus down. On the third day after the crucifixion God, the heavenly Father, raised Jesus to life again.

'Christians can share in the forgiveness and in the hope of God's presence with us here on earth, and in a sure future after we die,' I explained. 'That's what your brother means.'

Emily listened intently, but although she was intrigued, she wasn't convinced. 'I'm not even sure there is a God,' she said.

I remember smiling and rather cheekily replying, 'That's OK. He knows He exists and so do I. But I'd rather you find Him for yourself, than have me try to convince you – is that OK? Do you have a Bible?'

'No, I have never even seen a Bible,' said Emily.

After returning to my office, I brought back a copy of the Bible in a translation that did not have all the *thee*s and *thou*s of the early English versions. 'This is a gift for you, Emily.'

As Emily looked at her new Bible for the first time I explained a little about the book. 'The Bible is split into two major parts called the Old Testament (meaning 'agreement' or 'will') and the New Testament. The Old

Testament, mostly written originally in Hebrew, was written over hundreds of years. It tells the history of God with the people of Israel before the time of Jesus Christ. The New Testament was mostly written in the common trade language of the day, which was Greek. The New Testament begins with four different accounts of the life, death and resurrection of Jesus Christ (the Messiah) and what follows are insights into the early years of the Christian Church. The New Testament includes letters written to encourage and teach the early Christians in a hostile world.

'In the original languages there were no chapters or verses (the smaller sections in each chapter) in the Bible. These were added to help the reader find their place more easily.' I showed Emily how this worked.

'You said you really wanted to know whether there is a God and whether He loves you personally. Well, here is what I suggest you do,' I encouraged her. 'Why not start with the New Testament book written by Mark. It is the shortest account of the life of Jesus Christ. I recommend you read, say, about one chapter a day and think about it. But before you read, here is an important prayer to pray: "God, if You are there and if You love me like Ron has said, show me so I know…"'

Emily broke in and said, 'Yes, I can do that.'

Impressed by her enthusiasm, I continued, 'Wait, Emily. There's more.' To the prayer I'd suggested to her, I added: '… and I will do whatever You tell me.'

Emily thought for a few seconds and then replied, 'Yes. I will do that too.' Then she thanked me for my time, picked up her new Bible and left.

The next morning, I had a phone call from Emily, and it's this particular phone call that has made the lasting impression on me. After the usual pleasantries I asked, 'Why did you call?'

'Well, I've done it,' she replied enthusiastically.

'What have you done?'

'I am a Christian!' she said.

'Whoa! Slow down! Can you please explain to me what has happened?'

'Well,' she said, 'last night after I arrived home I did what you said. I prayed that prayer and I began reading Mark's book, but I could not stop with just one chapter – I read it all. Then I read all the books by Matthew, Luke and John. Then I read Acts and the letter to Romans. I went back to the Old Testament and read Genesis and Exodus. I was stuck in Leviticus. After that I said, "God, I now know You are real and I give my life to You."'

Listening to her enthusiasm and sincerity, I knew she meant what she was saying but I recognised that this was only the first step in a long journey with her heavenly Father, just as a wedding is only the first step in a long, healthy marriage.

What was it that touched Emily so that she would respond like that?

While Emily's growing knowledge of the Bible was very important, alone it would not have been enough to trigger her response. We all read, see and hear many things every day. Some we accept as significant and trustworthy. Other news we simply don't believe and discard. There is also other information that may be confusing or that requires more thought before we can decide whether to accept or reject it.

With Emily, something was stirring within her spirit, deeper than what she was reading or thinking. This stirring touches our longings and fires us with hope that there is indeed a God who is real and who is searching for us, perhaps even more than we are searching for Him.

If Christianity is only about beliefs and behaviour then it is just another religion. *'Believe the right things and do the right things.'* The words Emily read touched something deeper than her intellect and her behaviour. She was drawn to the character of Jesus Christ and God the Father whom she confronted in the New Testament accounts and in other biblical writings. She found a profound ring of truth that opened her up to respond, not to the ideas and information alone, but to the person behind the ideas. Christians would say that this awareness comes from the Holy Spirit, who is at work in the seeking person's inner being.

True Christian faith is always in a person, in Jesus Christ, the Son of God. It is a response to His invitation to enter a relationship with our creator, our heavenly Father, allowing Him to enter and guide our lives. Because God is essentially a spiritual being, He knows us intimately and is able to meet us in that deep human part that some call the human spirit. Undoubtedly, this is what occurred with Emily.

If you're thinking, as Emily did before her discovery, 'I don't believe any of this', then that is certainly your rightful choice – but if you are at all curious or eager to find out for yourself, I encourage you to begin the journey of seeking God for yourself. You could follow the steps that Emily did. Alternatively, you may know people you trust who are followers of Jesus with whom you can talk and discuss openly and honestly. In the end, your next steps are yours to decide.

But don't rush the process. Some people find their relationship with God develops slowly over months or even years. Second, don't be hurried along by well-meaning Christians. You alone will be aware of the right time for you to make this life-changing decision.

It is my strong belief that we are not meant to live life alone. We need God and we need others. Relationships are a key characteristic of what defines us as human beings. The battering and bruising of past experiences make individuals shy away from other human relationships. Sadly, many feel that perhaps God cannot be trusted either. Nevertheless we *are* relational beings.

There is, of course, a big problem: people are not perfect. This includes you and me. At their worst, people can be very damaging or hurtful to one another. It is no different for those of us who have made the decision to follow Jesus Christ. There are no perfect Christians. There's a saying that goes something like, 'If you find the perfect church, don't join it. You will ruin it.' So, if you connect with others on a journey with God, please don't expect them to be perfect!

In preparation for the Easter Sunday service a few years ago, some of the more creative people at my church decided to make a large wooden cross for the stage, and attach small mirrors to it to reflect the spotlights. Someone later suggested breaking the mirrors before sticking them onto the cross. There were many pieces of all shapes and sizes. It was quite the jigsaw puzzle, and the task took much longer than the original idea would have. But it was worth it. As the white spotlights hit the broken pieces of mirror at that Easter service, the light being reflected from both the smooth surfaces and the cracks, blended into a stunning and very thought-provoking image. People were moved to tears as they looked at the brokenness on the cross and were aware of their own weaknesses and pain. They were reminded that even though each one of them was imperfect, together in relationship they could present a beautiful and powerful message of what it means to be forgiven and included in the family of God.

If you begin a journey with Jesus, you won't find perfect people – but you will need others to support and encourage you on your journey. You will not get far in your relationship with Jesus by simply turning up at a church service week after week, and just sitting in a seat. Find what works for you – what style of worship and teaching helps you to engage and go deeper with your faith. Get stuck in to church community life – walk with others, and let them teach you, too. Whatever your next steps, my prayer is that what you have read will encourage you to search for God, so that you may be found by the Father who loves you best.

10

For the road...

'There's nothing like the written Word of God for showing you the way to salvation through faith in Christ Jesus. Every part of Scripture is God-breathed and useful one way or another– showing us truth, exposing our rebellion, correcting our mistakes, training us to live God's way.'

2 Timothy 3:17 (*The Message*)

Deciding to become a Christian or find out more about Jesus doesn't mean you're left to figure it all out for yourself, with just a dusty old Bible and a few books to help you. There are a number of resources out there, both written and in audio-visual forms, to help you get your head around some of these questions a bit more, or to go deeper with your thinking. And you don't have to jump straight in with the heavy stuff either.

Bibles

Our experience of reading the Bible can radically vary from one translation to another. If you really want to get your teeth into the meaning and context, a good Study Bible (the NIV comes highly recommended) might be really beneficial to your understanding. Alternatively, there are more 'creative' paraphrases out there that can really help bring the language to life (such as *New Living* (NLT), *The Message* and *The Voice* translations). I'd recommend reading these alongside a more traditional translation at some point in time, however, so that you can compare and consolidate your understanding.

Print Bibles

Eugene H. Peterson (ed.), *The Message Remix: The Bible in Contemporary Language* (Colorado Springs, CO, USA: NavPress, 2006)

The Holy Bible, New International Version, NIV (London: Hodder & Stoughton, 2011)

The Voice Bible (Nashville, TN, USA: Thomas Nelson, 2012)

New Living Translation, NLT (Carol Stream, IL, USA: Tyndale House Foundation, 2015)

Digital Bibles

A number of Bible reading apps are now available for smart devices, and many of them will allow you to select your preferred translation whenever you like. Olive Tree Bible+ (HarperCollins Christian Publishing, Inc.) comes highly recommended, and is free to download.

Books

Should you wish to continue your reading around faith-related subjects, here are some books that people in the UK and elsewhere have found helpful.

God

Timothy Keller, *Making Sense of God: An Invitation to the Sceptical* (London: Hodder, 2016)
Philip Yancey, *The Jesus I Never Knew* (Grand Rapids, MI, USA: Zondervan, 1998)

Purpose and Identity

Dave Smith, *Transformed Life* (Farnham: CWR, 2014)
Rick Warren, *The Purpose Driven Life* (Grand Rapids, MI, USA: Zondervan, 2002)

Christianity

Francis Chan, *Crazy Love: Overwhelmed by a Relentless God* (Colorado Springs, CO, USA: David C. Cook, 2013)
C.S. Lewis, *Mere Christianity* (New York: HarperCollins, 2001)
J.I. Packer, *Knowing God* (London: Hodder & Stoughton, 2004)

Prayer

Pete Greig, *God On Mute: Engaging the Silence of Unanswered Prayer* (Ventura, CA, USA: Regal Books, 2007)
Timothy Keller, *Prayer: Experiencing Awe and Intimacy with God* (New York: Penguin, 2014)

Courses

I hope that you will find a warm welcome at any church you visit, but there are several courses run by local churches that help answer questions about Jesus, faith and the meaning of life.

The Alpha Course

Originally developed in the 1990s as a brief introduction to Christianity, Alpha has since been used by millions of people all over the world. It's a friendly, informal 12-week course that takes place in a café-style environment – with food, a short talk about one of the key themes of the Christian faith, followed by group discussion and space to ask any questions you have.

Churches all over the country run Alpha courses regularly – and it's free! To find out more, visit **www.alpha.org**

Christianity Explored

Much like Alpha, Christianity Explored introduces you to the gospel of Jesus through seven sessions of Bible study. There's lots of information about the course (as well as other helpful resources) available at **www.christianityexplored.org**

Discipleship Explored

For those who have already started their Christian journey and want to go a bit deeper with their faith, this is a great series of group Bible studies that dig into some of the teaching of the New Testament, all about living out the Christian life. For more information, visit **www.ceminist ries.org**

Emily's prayer...

You might be wondering about your next step towards finding God for yourself.

If you want to take a leap of faith like Emily, and pray the words she prayed, here they are again:

God, if You are there and if You love me, show me so I know and I will do whatever You tell me. Amen.

May you find peace, security, hope and blessing as you continue your journey of discovering your way to your heavenly Father – your way home.

'Real stories about the ups and downs of trying to walk in Jesus' footsteps through daily life'
GRAHAM KENDRICK
the way
Living the Beatitudes today
CARL BEECH
FOREWORD BY ANDY HAWTHORNE
CARL BEECH The Way CWR